The Price of Stone

also by Richard Murphy

SAILING TO AN ISLAND
(1963)

THE BATTLE OF AUGHRIM
(1968)

HIGH ISLAND
(1974)

SELECTED POEMS
(1979)

RICHARD MURPHY

The Price of Stone

faber and faber
LONDON · BOSTON

First published in 1985
by Faber and Faber Limited
3 Queen Square London WC1N 3AU

Filmset by Wilmaset
Birkenhead Merseyside
Printed in Great Britain by
Whitstable Litho Ltd
Whitstable Kent

British Library Cataloguing in Publication Data

Murphy, Richard
The price of stone
I. Title
821'.914 PR6063.U735
ISBN 0–571–13568–4

TO
DENNIS O'DRISCOLL

Contents

Acknowledgements 15

PART I

Moonshine 19
Care 20
Trouvaille 22
Mary Ure 23
Shelter 24
Niches 25
Swallows 26
Stone Mania 27
Husbandry 28
A Nest in a Wall 29
Tony White 30
Tony White at Inishbofin 31
Bookcase for the Oxford English Dictionary 32
Morning Call 33
Arsonist 34
Elixir 35
Amsterdam 36
Altar 37
Displaced Person 38
Amazement 39
Visiting Hour 40

PART II: THE PRICE OF STONE

Folly 43
Lead Mine Chimney 44
Portico 45
Nelson's Pillar 46

Wellington Testimonial 47
Georgian Tenement 48
Gym 49
Knockbrack 50
Ice Rink 51
Carlow Village Schoolhouse 52
Roof-Tree 53
Red Bank Restaurant 54
Little Barn 55
Connemara Quay 56
Birth Place 57
Queen of the Castle 58
Liner 59
Planter Stock 60
Family Seat 61
Rectory 62
Letterfrack Industrial School 63
Baymount 64
Canterbury Cathedral 65
Choir School 66
Suntrap 67
Gate Lodge 68
Milford: East Wing 69
Carlyon Bay Hotel 70
Wellington College 71
Oxford Staircase 72
Convenience 73
Lecknavarna 74
Killary Hostel 75
Waterkeeper's Bothy 76
Kylemore Castle 77
Tony White's Cottage 78
Pier Bar 79
Miner's Hut 80
Hexagon 81

New Forge 82
Cottage for Sale 83
Horse-Drawn Caravan 84
Old Dispensary 85
Chalet 86
Prison 87
Wattle Tent 88
Newgrange 89
Friary 90
Beehive Cell 91
Natural Son 92

Acknowledgements

Grateful acknowledgements are made to the American Irish Foundation for the 1983 Literary Award; to Marten Toonder and the Arts Council of Ireland for the Marten Toonder Award; to the Arts Council of Great Britain for a bursary; to Aosdána; to Rose Saul Zalles and the Catholic University of America for their sponsorship; to the Cornamona Press of Amsterdam for a limited edition of 'Care'; to the Gallery Press of Dublin for a limited edition of 'Niches'; and to the editors of *Bananas* (London), *Digraphe* (Paris), *Grand Street* (New York), *The First Ten Years* (Dublin), *Helix* (Australia), the *Irish Literary Supplement* (New York), the *Irish Times*, the *Irish University Review*, the *London Magazine*, the *London Review of Books*, the *New Statesman*, the *New York Review of Books*, *Oxford Poetry*, *Poetry Australia*, *Poetry Ireland Review*, *Ramp* (Holland), *Sewanee Review*, the *Times Literary Supplement* and the *Sunday Tribune*; also to the BBC, RTE and the Australian Broadcasting Commission.

PART I

Moonshine

To think
I must be alone:
To love
We must be together.

I think I love you
When I'm alone
More than I think of you
When we're together.

I cannot think
Without loving
Or love
Without thinking.

Alone I love
To think of us together:
Together I think
I'd love to be alone.

Care

Kidded in April above Glencolumbkille
On a treeless hill backing north, she throve
Sucking milk off heather and rock, until

I came with children to buy her. We drove
South, passing Drumcliff. Restless in the car,
Bleating, she gulped at plastic teats we'd shove

Copiously in her mouth. Soon she'd devour
Whatever we'd give. Prettily she poked
Her gypsy head with hornbuds through barbed wire

To nip off pea-tops, her fawn pelt streaked
With Black Forest shadow and Alpine snow.
I stalled her wildness in a pen that locked.

She grew tame and fat, fed on herbs I knew
Her body needed. We ransacked Kylemore
To bring her oakleaf, ivy and bark to chew.

I gutted goatbooks, learning how to cure
Fluke, pulpy kidney, black garget, louping ill:
All my attention bled to cope with her.

No commonage to roam unfenced, no hill
Where she could vanish under a dark cloud
To forage with a puck-led flock: but the dull

Grind of small children bucketing her food,
Yelling across a yard. Out in a forest
She would have known a bad leaf from a good.

Here, captive to our taste, she'd learnt to trust
The petting hand with crushed oats, or a new
Mash of concentrates, or sweet bits of waste.

So when a child mistook a sprig of yew
And mixed it with her fodder, she descried
No danger: we had tamed her instinct too.

Whiskey, white of egg, linseed oil, we tried
Forcing down antidotes. Nothing would do.
The children came to tell me when she died.

Trouvaille

This root of bog-oak the sea dug up she found
Poking about, in old age, and put to stand
Between a snarling griffin and a half-nude man
Moulded of lead on my chimney-piece.
It looks like a heron rising from a pond,
Feet dipped in brown trout water,
Head shooting arrow-sharp into blue sky.

'What does it remind you of?' she wanted to know.
I thought of trees in her father's demesne
Levelled by chainsaws;
Bunches of primroses I used to pick
Before breakfast, hunting along a limestone lane,
To put at her bedside before she woke;
And all my childhood's broken promises.

No, no! It precedes alphabets,
Planted woods, or gods.
Twisted and honed as a mind that never forgets
It lay dead in bog acids, undecayable:
Secretively hardening in a womb of moss, until
The peat burnt off, a freak tide raised
The feathered stick she took to lure me home.

Mary Ure

Bare feet she dips across my boat's blue rail
In the ocean as we run under full white summer sail.
The cold spray kisses them. She's not immortal.

Sitting in her orchard she reads 'Lady Lazarus'
Aloud rehearsing, when her smallest child lays
Red peonies in her lap with tender apologies.

She walks by Lough Mask in a blue silk gown
So thin the cloudy wind is biting to the bone
But she talks as lightly as if the sun shone.

Shelter

Girl with a sheaf of rye straw in your arms
How much you carry from a loaded trailer
Parked at the door in a stray sunny shaft
At the tail end of summer, deep into the barn
To store for thatch, if ever we get the weather
Or the time, before winter sets in, how much
You help me, child, in the hour after school,
Hour of your release, face wet with tears
That well up out of a cruelty done to you,
Bruise marks around your lips, a speechless harm,
How much you help me to make the dark inside
Glitter with sheaves bound firm to keep out storm.
Hear how they rustle as we lay them down:
Their broken heads are thrashed clean of grain.

Niches

Lovers I've lost are sleeping in the house I've left
To live alone in a cave with two glass entrances,
A skylight in the roof over a chair that broods
At the bottom of a well of sunshine on clear days,
Or a pit of night kept warm by a peat fire
When hailstones jitter, as now with a northerly gale
Squalling through cracks in my costly new shell:
While two calm urns of white Cycladic clay
Stand silently still in niches I drew last summer
In the random warm granite of my chimney breast.
A woman threw them lovingly, glazed them in tears,
Fired them one sleepless night, and put them here to stay
For ever. Now she's dismantled her wheel and gone.
Niched above my head I'll keep her bone-ash jars.

Swallows

She wades through wet rushes,
Long autumn grass,
Over rusty barbed wire
And stone walls that collapse,

With a black rubber torch
Flickering on and off,
After midnight, to reach
A shed with a tin roof.

She lifts away door boards –
O sweet herbal hay!
Her beam dazzles birds
She can't identify.

Timorous wings in wormy rafters
Flap to get out.
Then she spots in a light shaft
A red boot unlaced.

The flock's tremor increases
In her torch's coop.
Where is he? She sees
A white arm sticking up.

Stone Mania

How much it hurts me to tidy up when all my papers are
heaped on the desk in a three-month mess,
To regain control of this drift of days I've lost in
my passion for building in granite,
And face the bills I must pay by leaving the house
that has cost me too much to enlarge,
Where I passed the time too quickly preparing a place for
the future to work within soundproof walls,
So never had a moment in the present for writing about
the moments that were passing away:
How much it hurts to see the destruction that all good
building, even the best, must cause,
Not only the hedges that had to be first cut down
before the foundations were dug,
But deeper cuts through veins in the mind that carried
the blood of memory through the brain:
How much it hurts me to have neglected all this summer
the friends whom I might have seen,
But for my mad obsession of building more rooms
to entertain them in time to come:
Because these times are apt to elude us, we die, or our
friends drop dead before we can say
I'd love you to see and enjoy the house whose construction
has kept us entirely apart.

Husbandry

Sheep like to graze on headlands
High up looking down on a raging sea.
It makes me dizzy to watch
An old ewe
Leaning over the edge to reach with her black mouth
A tuft of grass fine as hair.
I'd have to crawl there clutching frail stems.

How many of the flock fall
Dashed on to rocks or drowned in surf
To satisfy a peculiar hunger.
No soft herb
Pleases them as much as the spikes of gorse.
If I were their shepherd
I'd put them to fatten in a small safe paddock.

A Nest in a Wall

Smoky as peat your lank hair on my pillow
Burns like a tinker's fire in a mossy ditch.
Before I suffocate, let me slowly suck
From your mouth a tincture of mountain ash,
A red infusion of summer going to seed.
Ivy clumps loosen the stonework of my heart.
Come like a wood pigeon gliding there to roost!

I float a moment on a gust sighing for ever
Gently over your face where two swans swim.
Let me kiss your eyes in the slate-blue calm
Before their Connemara clouds return.
A spancelled goat bleats in our pleasure ground.
A whippet snarls on its chain. The fire dies out.
Litter of rags and bottles in the normal rain.

Your country and mine, love, can it still exist?
The unsignposted hawthorn lane of your body
Leads to my lichenous walls and gutted house.
Your kind of beauty earth has almost lost.
Although we have no home in the time that's come,
Coming together we live in our own time.
Make your nest of moss like a wren in my skull.

Tony White

1930–1976

Growing, he saw his friends increase
Their incomes, houses, families,
And saw this growth as a disease
Nothing but unpossessive love could cure.
Possessing nothing, he was not possessed
By things or people, as we are.
His granite chimney breast
Warmed friend or stranger at its open fire.
There was no air
Too foul for him to breathe, no pit
Too dark to enter, yet
His very breathing made the foul air pure,
His presence made the darkest day feel clear.

He lived at the hub and not the rim
Of time. Within himself he moved
Deeper towards dangerous ideas he loved
To moot with bodily risk:
Flying too close to the sun's disk,
Sailing at night over a coral reef,
Ghosting a thief's life.
Since he's gone
No words of mine can rivet him to one
Role of some forty-nine he used to play
For pleasure more than pay.
Because his kind of love taught me to live
His dying I forgive.

Tony White at Inishbofin

1959

With a lobster pot for a chair
And a fishbox for a table
He'd sacrificed a plausible career
On the London stage to live near
The sea in a bare room
Far from home
To become on the lips of islanders a fable.

In an old pair of black jeans
Threadbare though tautly darned
By himself needling with a woman's patience
Buckled in a looted Hun's
Eagle and swastika belt
Disguised he felt
Reborn as a fisherman whose craft he learned.

From an off-white Aran sweater
Knit by his neighbour's wife
His dark face opened like a long love-letter
That makes a forlorn reader
Revive with a gust of hope
While he moused rope
For crayfish traps with a horn gutting knife.

Through small panes of cobwebbed glass
Across a limewashed stone sill
He hauled in shoals of riffled sun to please
Only a few friends like us
Because it was his style
To play as well
Carrying a creel on his back or Coriolanus.

Bookcase for the Oxford English Dictionary

All the words I need
Stored like seed in a pyramid
To bring back from the dead your living shade
Lie coffined in this thing of wood you made
Of solid pine mortised and glued
Not long before you died.

Words you'll never read
Are good for nothing but to spread
Your greater love of craft in word and deed,
A gift to make your friends' desires succeed
While inwardly with pain you bled
To keep your own pride hid.

Morning Call

Up from the trawlers in the fishdock they walk to my house
On high-soled clogs, stepping like fillies back from a forge
Newly shod, to wake me at sunrise from a single bed
With laughter peeling skin from a dream ripening on the mossy
Branches of my head – 'Let us in! Let us in!' – and half-naked
I stumble over a floor of heaped paper to open my door of glass
To a flood that crosses the threshold, little blue waves

Nudging each other, dodging rocks they've got to leap over,
Freshening my brackish pools, to tell me of 'O such a night
Below in the boats!' 'We can't go home! What *will* they say?'
Can I think of a lie to protect them from God only knows
What trouble this will cause, what rows? 'We'll run away
And never come back!' – till they flop into black armchairs,
Two beautiful teenage girls from a tribe of tinkers,

Lovely as seals wet from fishing, hauled out on a rock
To dry their dark brown fur glinting with scales of salmon
When the spring tide ebbs. This is their everlasting day
Of being young. They bring to my room the sea's iodine odour
On a breeze of voices ruffling my calm as they comb their long
Hair tangled as weed in a rockpool beginning to settle clear.
Give me the sea-breath from your mouths to breathe a while!

Arsonist

The summer visitors have gone.
Rain blathers at the glass.
He drifts alone
On the soundwaves of his vacant house.

So firm his tongued and grooved oak floors!
By his building he's possessed.
His dark teak doors
Creak as they close him in his past.

Each random stone made integral
Has bonded him with debt.
All he can feel
Is a dying to get rid of it.

With craft to burn, how could he use
Control to lose control,
To spark a blaze
Spontaneous and elemental?

Fire would transmute his home in hours
To a foetiferous void,
A mould that flowers
Gravid with fronds of gutter lead.

Elixir

Turning a stone house into seven figures
Transported him to money's clean cold alp
To hang-glide on a market's thermal rigours
Learning new ways to corner, hedge or scalp.

Turning a copper nail that tightly gripped
A green slate on his roof to daily bread
Made him afraid to eat when sterling dipped
And meat cost more than door locks or sheet lead.

Turning a life's work into stocks and shares
Converted him to shirk the tears and shocks
Of love, rid of laborious household cares
And freed him to buy sex on piers and docks.

Turning old granite walls to bars of gold
Amassed his fears of sudden falls in one
Commodity. When all his wealth was told
It filled a vault with bone-dry speculation.

Turning his home into a foreign room
Replete with art to beat inflation chilled
His heart to zero. In that ice-bound tomb
He housed immortal seed unsowed, untilled.

Amsterdam

Money was evil:
Therefore he locked up large sums of it in gold,
In ships and warehouses,
Polders and dikes,
To hold back the leviathan and the flood,
To stop it corrupting poor people
Who might have bought luxuries,
Drugs and whores,
Or wasted their lives enjoying themselves.

How his capital has grown!
Where he used to sit at night in his room
With no curtains drawn
To show next-door neighbours
His gloomy interior had nothing evil to hide,
A girl from the Far East with her breasts bare
Sits stoned in red light
And a strange greasy flood
Leaches into her parlour with money to burn.

Altar

Blocking the way to get behind the house
To climb crooked stone steps to see the view
A huge grey granite boulder lay. With you
To help, I'd shift the obstacle with ease.

Was it a mass-rock blessed in penal days
Better left undisturbed? Too near the wall
It made our bedroom weep. Too flat to roll
It caught a bulldozer between two trees.

A wise old mason told us to use fire
And water. One calm Sunday we piled coal
To heaven. Then doused the hot slab from a pool.
Not a seam cracked. Instead, we'd fouled the air.

Chagrined, we tried digging a deep wide pit;
Eased down the bald obtruder; buried it.

Displaced Person

Those years ago, when I made love to you,
With fears I was afraid you knew,
To grow strong I'd pretend to be
A boy I'd loved, loving yourself as me.
I played his part so open-eyed that you
Believed my artful ploy was true.
To show I'd nothing false to hide
And make you feel the truth of love I lied.

The love of truth made me confess, and died
Exposing my hermetic guide,
A youth found loitering in the mart
Of memory's torn-down inner-city heart.
I feel betrayed by dead words that decide
If head or tail be certified.
Dear girl, come back and take a new
Lover in me, let him make love to you.

Amazement

These are the just
Who kill unjustly men they call unjust.

These are the pure in heart
Who see God smeared in excrement on walls.

These are the patriots
Who starve to give the ravening media food.

These are the martyrs
Who die for a future buried in the past.

These are the sacrifice
A word imprisoned and a word could save.

Visiting Hour

How can I comfort you? What can I say?
You seem so far away, though near me now,
Sedated in that iron bed
Behind a curtain I'm afraid to draw:
With languished head
Propped on a pillow, mute and weak.
Would it be better not to speak?

Do you remember the day
We drifted west of Cleggan Bay
In the slack of tide, a fish on every hook:
The crossed lines and the lost
Leads, and seagulls scrawling around the mast
That listed while waves yeasted over a rock:
The gutted pollock gasping on our deck?

At least your poetry will stay unblurred.
Stuck with needles in this ward,
No peasant shoulders to support your feet,
You lie and fret. Work incomplete.
Tubes in your throat. And this is you,
Who put flesh into words that can't renew
The life you lavished making them ring true.

PART II

The Price of Stone

Folly

I rise from a circle standing on a square
And cock my dunce's cap at the firmament
Keeping my ignorance tapered to a clear
Sugarloaf point above the dark green ferment.

A lord's pride made me to relieve the poor
With heavy work lifting my spire, and the rich
With light step ascending my gazebo stair
To admire the land they owned and wish for more.

My form is epicene: male when the gold
Seed of the sun comes melting through my skin
Of old grey stucco: female when the mould
Of moonlight makes my witch-pap cone obscene.

My four doors bricked up against vandals, still
Tumescent, scrawled with muck, I crest the hill.

Lead Mine Chimney

Pointlessly standing up to make a pointed
Remark on a skyline everyone can see
Not puffing smoke out any more, disjointed
By age, I speak of cut stone symmetry.

Remember when you look at my cold grey stack
I took the heart from oakwoods to smelt ore,
Made people richer, poorer. Now I lack
The guts to pour out sulphur and hot air.

When you've poked your head inside my bevelled flue,
Inhaled a sooty chill of hollowness,
You'll know I've lost the fury to renew
The furnace at my root, all that foul stress.

Clearly I'll go on uttering, while I may,
In granite style, with not a word to say.

Portico

A dark headland hangs in a beady noose
Of mercury vapour across a bay of mud.
All night, solitary shadows of men cruise
My concrete cloister, ghosts questing blood.

I perch on rocks by the cineritious sea
Fossilized in decay: no painted porch
For a stoic mind, no shore temple of Shiva,
But a new kind of succursal, deviate church.

My spumy grotto's hooded devotees,
Sucked in a black hole that the sea has scoured,
Perform on flutes groping, mute melodies
With a seedy touch of ithyphallic art.

My hymns are hog-snorts, squealing bottle-glass
Screwed underfoot, a wave's foghorn caress.

Nelson's Pillar

My duty done, I rose as a Doric column
Far from at home, planted to reach the sky;
A huge stake in the crossed heart of a glum
Garrison city overlooked by my blind eye.

One-armed on a cold square abacus to rule
The waves, I never controlled the verminous
Poor beggars round my plinth, schooled to rebel.
I was loved well as a tramway's terminus.

Who cares, now, what good masons carved my four
Sea victories in granite from Golden Hill?
When masked men cracked my head off, the blast wore
Red, white and blue in a flash of puerile skill.

Dismasted and dismissed, without much choice,
Having lost my touch, I'll raise my chiselled voice.

Wellington Testimonial

Needling my native sky over Phoenix Park
I obelize the victory of wit
That let my polished Anglo-Irish mark
Be made by Smirke, as a colossal spit.

Properly dressed for an obsolete parade,
Devoid of mystery, no winding stair
Threading my unvermiculated head,
I've kept my feet, but lost my nosy flair.

My life was work: my work was taking life
To be a monument. The dead have won
Capital headlines. Look at Ireland rife
With maxims: need you ask what good I've done?

My sole point in this evergreen oak aisle
Is to maintain a clean laconic style.

Georgian Tenement

The high court of dry rot, after a long
Unreportable session behind airtight doors,
Has mouthed a verdict. Rafters know what's wrong.
Death and cremation. Up with my soft floors.

I've got to be rebuilt. Some new, banal
Office block is decreed to fill my place.
The whores under the trees by the canal
Increase their turnover while I lose face.

Young lovers of old structures, you who squat
To keep my form intact, when guards arrive
With riot gear and water gun, we cannot
Under such tonnage of cracked slate survive.

Would that your free hands in my spongy wood
Could cure fungosity, make my flaws good.

Gym

Vice-regal walls dominate the back street
Where men, succumbing to my spurious name
For body culture, enter in retreat
From words that shame, to act a heartless mime.

Discreetly couched, taking no verbal risk,
Ingled in clutches masked by sauna steam,
Nude club members, immune from women, bask
In tableaux mixed with musak, cocaine, jism.

See how my fabric, full of cock and bull,
Grotesquely free, though ruled by symmetry,
Lays you in some small penetralian cell
To come to grief, past all immunity.

The powers that be, served covertly by aids,
Strip to the bone your skin-deep masquerades.

Knockbrack

When driven to explore a strange blind alley
First clambering footloose up a speckled hill
You gambled on rare views of infilled valley,
Blossom of Chinese tang on a thorny grill.

Coming to speculate, you stayed for good:
Your fortune in the gold market of whins.
Avuncular pines admonished you to brood
On dark tale ends with woodcut colophons.

A spirited father walked barefoot to Rome:
A son died sniffing glue. Nobody lasted.
As well finished as rifle bolts at the Somme
My door locks made you feel safely invested.

Grey granite cropped up an archaic head
To check your feet, your line of living dead.

Ice Rink

Reflections of a spotlit mirror-ball,
Casting a light net over a pearl pond
In oval orbits, magnify my haul
Of small fry at a disco, coiled in sound.

On anticlockwise tracks, all shod with steel,
Initiates feel exalted; starlets glide
To cut more ice with convoluted skill
Practising tricks that lure them to backslide.

Their figure-carving feet have chased my skin
With puckish onslaught. Gloss they vitiate
For pure fun, when they joust through thick and thin,
Vanishes under frost, a hoar-stone slate.

Midnight, my crushed face melts in a dead heat:
Old scores ironed out, tomorrow a clean sheet.

Carlow Village Schoolhouse

Much as you need a sonnet house to save
Your muse, while sifting through our foetid pits
Of blighted roots, he needed my firm, grave
Façade, to be freed from bog-dens and sod-huts.

Such symmetry he gained from me, you got
By birth, given his names. Twenty poor scholars,
Birched if they uttered Irish words, he taught
To speak like you, faults notched on wooden collars.

We faced the crossroads four square. Where I stood
Is void now, so be fair. Not forced to sip
The cauldron soup with undying gratitude,
Would *you* have chosen to board a coffin-ship?

All you've seen is his proud clean signature
As a wedding witness that worst famine year.

Roof-Tree

After you brought her home with your first child
How did you celebrate? Not with a poem
She might have loved, but orders to rebuild
The house. Men tore me open, room by room.

Your daughter's cries were answered by loud cracks
Of hammers stripping slates; the clawing down
Of dozed rafters; dull, stupefying knocks
On walls. Proudly your hackwork made me groan.

Your greed for kiln-dried oak that could outlast
Seven generations broke her heart. My mind
You filled with rot-proof hemlock at a cost
That killed her love. The dust spread unrefined.

To renovate my structure, which survives,
You flawed the tenderest movement of three lives.

Red Bank Restaurant

Was it a taste for black sole on the bone
Brought you two down from your mountain farm one night
To meet that Faustian guest, whose writing shone
In her sight, eating devilled prawn by candlelight?

Le sang du pauvre, he quipped, gulping more wine
You'd pay for, squandering the blood-money received
From her pilot brother's crash. Richly malign
Elevation of the hostess he'd conceived.

His cruiser eyes, when not nailed to her cross
By mother wit, fled exiled through the bar:
Soon to be reconciled, screened by clear glass,
As he smiled at his cold brilliance mirrored there.

All you could think was that your sloe hedge field
Would need spike-harrowing for a better yield.

Little Barn

It's not my place to speak more than I must
Whether of bloodstock, interest rates or corn.
She feels enclosed inside a lacquered nest
Of Chinese boxes, sealed from your concern.

I've been converted to increase the rent
Between us, cornered in a stable yard;
Spruce enclave, heavenly views; a fortress meant
To keep out southern storms; flint cobbles tarred.

Those Russian dolls her infant son and yours
Breaks open as a blue-eyed Williamite
He puts together again without more tears.
Your customs are so strange we can't unite.

She moulds the clay and fires the waterpot
He balances, authorized by you or not.

Connemara Quay

I should have done this, that and all those things
Goodwill intended when I was designed
To end the poor land's hunger. Failure brings
Catches that slip through nets too close to mind.

Men stood me up here, promising that I'd be
Their godsend: ocean would provide more food.
The green earth should have married the grey sea,
But fell foul of her storms, her moody tide.

Attached by strings of warps to my stone head,
Fine wooden craft came, to be overcome
By torpor. Keels took root in silt of seabed,
Ribbed frames rotted in a frayed hemp dream.

You played in these hulks half a century ago.
What did you think you might do? Now you know.

Birth Place

I'd been expecting death by absentee
Owner's decay, or fire from a rebel match.
Too many old relations I'd seen die
In the same bedroom made me scared to watch.

Between her cries, I heard carts trundling books
Gone mouldy to a bonefire in the yard.
Wild bees in my roof were filling up their wax
Hexagonals from our lime trees, working hard.

A boy led a pony round and round a small
Hedged pond, pumping spring water for her use.
And then your birth cry came, piercing through wall
Behind wall. The sun transfigured all of us.

It shone like honey on doorsteps of brown bread.
The August evening kissed her worn out head.

Queen of the Castle

Her face is gone from me. Only her voice
Will spring to mind as water underground
Near an abysmal swallow-hole, the place
Where toddling after a ball you almost drowned.

A dirty rascal egged you on, then dug
His foot in your back. A giant grabbed your hair
Standing on end, with a strong gardener's tug
To root you out, and shake you in pure air.

You breathed her love away like a dandelion head
In my field of vision, looking all day long
For your duck, wandering astray. Is she dead?
Gorged by the fox? You made such a sad song.

Listen to me! She's coming back. O look!
Here, with seven ducklings. You could write a book.

Liner

I'm steaming home, ploughing your peace of mind,
With the bow-wave poise of a duchess coaching through
Her deep blue shire; buoyantly waterlined;
Brass port-holes burnished by my lascar crew.

Dolphins precede us, playing for good schools
With somersaulting skills. Petrels astern
Writhe in our screwed up wake. Obeying the rules
You're learning to spin rope quoits, turn by turn.

Child, when you've sailed half way around the world
And found that home is like a foreign country,
Think how I've had to keep an ironclad hold
On your belongings, not to lose heart at sea.

The gong is ringing. Here comes your ice-cream.
There's more to mind than raising heads of steam.

Planter Stock

People look up to me, though I'm falling down,
And wonder why a monkey-puzzle tree
Chose to ascend from seaweed a hard mountain
Whose gorse-gold standard plunges into scree.

I love old watercolours curlews paint
With iodine on a quill down a glen's throat;
Deplore the weather's poor mouth complaint;
Wear fuchsia tweed, an ancient ivy coat.

Can't you eat rabbit? Does it make you sick
To find your father's gun-shots in your meat,
Or touch a trout he's caught? You ought to like
Wearing an Eton collar; you look sweet.

All the roots that would pack inside a tea chest
Came home when we retired from the Far East.

Family Seat

Clouds make me look as though I disapprove
Of everyone. You know that grim, grey face
Of limestone cut by famine workmen. Love
Is never allowed to show it rules the place.

But love I took from a ruling family,
And gave them back a wealth of lovely things:
As a trout river talking with propriety
Through cockshoot woods, bailiffed by underlings.

Their silver knives adored their crested forks.
Blue-veiny hands, like yours, kept my clocks wound
On endless landings: others did good works
Like typing Braille. High walls surround my land.

They've all been buried in their name-proud vaults.
Paraplegics live here now, and love my faults.

Rectory

My porous rock foundations can't keep down
Rising damp from arcane rheumatic springs
That creep up walls. Wet plaster makes him frown,
As when her black dogs leap up, licking things.

She lets them loose. He's choked by a dog-collar.
Time's silver chain is hung on his clean breast.
They sniff at holy orders, flung in choler:
Scenting her cling of lavender, feel blessed.

He carpets boys like you for playing with fire.
Bitches on heat can make mixed marriages.
You're lockjawed by his chinwag. Jubilee year,
Have you no higher thoughts than dog-rampages?

Her pups retrieve your first poem: a dead duck
Stuffed with bay leaves. Page after page they pluck.

Letterfrack Industrial School

Bog-brown glens, mica schist rocks, waterfalls
Gulching down screes, a rain-logged mountain slope
With scrawny pine trees twisted by mad gales,
They see from my ball yard, and abandon hope.

Wild boys my workshops chasten and subdue
Learn here the force of craft. Few can escape
My rack of metal, wood, thread, hide: my screw
Of brotherhood: the penny stitched in a strap.

Podded in varnished pews, stunted in beds
Of cruciform iron, they bruise with sad, hurt shame:
Orphans with felons, bastards at loggerheads
With waifs, branded for life by a bad name.

One, almost hanged in my boot room, has run free
Dressed as a girl, saved by a thieving gypsy.

Baymount

Describe a gate lodge like a dragon's mouth
Taking in boys and parents with a grin;
Then spitting out the parents. Iron teeth
Close when the last proud vintage car has gone.

Start counting days of terminal homesickness
Minus the love of those who left you here.
Draw six parallel lines cut quick across
Two flaming circles. Be prepared for war.

Stand up, our youngest new boy, what's-your-name!
Your uncle ate a wineglass in his mess
At Woolwich, and Dobbs major a live worm
Washed down with ink. Prove you're no cowardly ass!

Open your mouth wide, and with one bite take
The candle burning on this tower of cake!

Canterbury Cathedral

What building tuned your ear for poetry? Mine,
You remember, trained your childhood voice that filled
My quire with a sharp sound. You poured in my fine
Keyed vaults the grains of song my stonework milled.

When Canon Crum took you to climb dim stairs
That spiralled into my cranium, did you dream
You'd found my brain, with its treadmill, slow repairs,
Refacing a gargoyle, splicing an oak beam?

Now, you've come back, not to sing the *Te Deum*
In my nave, but to retrieve from your song's ground
The love you gave me then. Above the triforium
It soared to reach martyrs in stained glass crowned.

'Nine o'clock on a clear night, and all's well'
You heard, as you fell asleep, with my curfew bell.

Choir School

Our mother Church raised me on Kentish flint
Foundations dug in the Black Prince's day.
Two lily-white boys from dissolute Ireland,
You starred with your brother in our passion play.

How could you reach Mr Knight's perfect pitch,
Control his organ stops, ten hands, four feet?
Good God! How could you score without a hitch
His music sheets, braced for a lofty treat?

'Glorious things' your ruff-necked voices rang
In Mr Poole's purple passage through Caen stone.
One Easter, despite Hitler's bombs, you sang
Our new Archbishop to St Augustine's throne.

You shared my dormer view. A fiendish power
Rained fire on us: God spared Bell Harry Tower.

Suntrap

One year at home under my flagging roof
During the war, learning and love made peace.
Like a bone-setting weaver's warp and woof
Your heart and mind were shuttled into place.

Verbs conjugating in my pleasure ground
Held the past present in contiguous time.
Here was the Bower of Bliss, painlessly scanned.
You found the oldest trees were best to climb.

No neutral motherland, my walled demesne,
In tilting you towards knight-errant books,
Groomed you to mount grand war-horses to gain
Rewards beyond my laurels, birches, oaks.

A peeled rush, dipped in tallow, carried light
From the dark ages, kissing you good night.

Gate Lodge

Two Irish yews, prickly green, poisonous,
Divide my entrance, tapering in trim gloom.
Old rookery buildings, pitch-pine resinous,
Wake up shell-shocked, welcoming you back home.

Barefoot a child skips from my hearth to touch
The wrought obsequious latch of lip-service;
Taking you in, between double gates, to reach
Beyond the ruts your mother's peerless place.

I face my forbear's relic, a neat sty
That hovelled with his brogue some grateful clod
Unearthed by famine; and I hear go by
Your souper choir school voice defrauding God.

Pigeon park, pheasant wood and snipe bog lie
Within my scope: your shotgun territory.

Milford: East Wing

Stiff to open, needing a gentleman's grasp
Or a strong young maid's, my hall door, tight in its frame
Of wood at the long lime avenue's end, would gasp
With delight if callers of the old calibre came.

No judder shook my back door's ease of pulling
Lame ducks in; tinkers with babies, diseased and poor,
For a bite to eat; mockery of the cook killing
A rat with a poker on the foul scullery floor.

If it heard a piano playing, or psalms being sung,
A goat used my study door to butt in, and lie
Sniffing your mother's foot, for devilment bleating
Low notes that made your voice break on high.

My postern had to be nailed up, ivy-bound,
To keep the farmyard out of the pleasure ground.

Carlyon Bay Hotel

Designed for luxury, commandeered to house
Your bombed out school, under Spartan rule I live
In a Cornish idyll, with high and mighty views:
Royal blue channel, Phoenician tin-veined cliff.

Don't you know there's a war? It's why you're here
Debarred from girls, a pup among top dogs.
Home is ninety days off, and you've no future
Hunting hares over treacherous Irish bogs.

Wing-collared Milner scholar, don't forget
Your gas mask, ration book, identity card.
My buckthorn wood hears inklings in the black-out.
Uncle Jack's killed in Africa. Work hard!

Your voice is breaking. Kneel, and be confirmed
By Truro's hands of clay. Do you feel transformed?

Wellington College

Fear makes you lock out more than you include
By tackling my red brick with Shakespeare's form
Of love poem, barracked here and ridiculed
By hearty boys, drilled to my square-toed norm.

Yet ushered in, through my roll of honour voice,
Cold baths in winter, field days on Bagshot Heath,
Poetry gives you unconscripted choice
Of strategies, renaissance air to breathe.

Your father's brother fell in the Great War,
Your mother's fell in this. You ate our salt.
Should you plead conscience when called up next year
Their greater love would find the gravest fault.

Weren't you born to command a regiment?
How selfishly you serve your own heart's bent.

Oxford Staircase

Going up a flight of stone at seventeen
In wartime, wearing thin your plodding soles
On coupons by degrees, you pass between
Dons' billowing gowns and chapel aureoles.

Brought to your knees by genuflectory prose –
C. S. Lewis, stoking the clinkered grate
Of lost causes, keeps you on your toes –
You're taught to criticize, but not create.

That numinous cloud of jovial pipe smoke round
His Tudor head, wraps you tongue-tied as bells
Before VE Day, taking steps to sound
The blissful city fraught with private hells.

A fellowship of bowls on the cloister lawn
Do you miss, old man? You slipped up, going down.

Convenience

The public servant of men's private parts,
Plain clothed in the underground below Eros,
With white glazed stalls, and see-through mirror arts,
I plumb our language empire's omphalos.

Your profane oracle, I speak through a crack
In a mental block, going far back to the year
You stood here, epicentred on the shock
Of gross accusation, quaking at words like queer.

I watched you face an absurd firing squad
Unbuttoning uniforms. I, too, had lost
My primal sense in the promiscuous crowd.
Detected, blackmailed, judged, you paid the cost.

A life sentence, ambiguously imposed,
Props you behind all kinds of bars, exposed.

Lecknavarna

Look where I'm stuck the wrong side of Lough Fee:
Bad road, no neighbours, in the squally shade
Of a bleak mountain. Yet you took to me
When young. What made you seek my solitude?

Did you need my poor virgin concrete shell
No family cared to live in, just to write
Poetry, worshipping my waterfall,
Abased in loneliness by lust at night?

Still flowing steadfast in a flagstone cleft
Of stunted alders clinging on, it pours
With resonant gravity, bringing the gift
Of widespread raindrops crafted to great force.

Hearing that strong cadence, you learned your trade
Concerned with song in endless falling, stayed.

Killary Hostel

The young have redressed my slated history
Nailed to this wild coast in the famished past
On a deep ocean inlet, and restored me
As their last outpost of folksong and feast.

Mackerel swim through my windows at high tide.
You blotted a blank page of lyrical youth
With epic faults in my loneliest interlude,
Hooked here in boyhood on the Tír na n-Óg myth.

Didn't you follow that exiled Austrian
Who stood on my murky lane with a walking-stick
Drawing diagrams for the birds to explain?
Sea-urchins mocked him with folkloric tricks.

He left, in my turf-shed rafters, a small sign
To question all our myths . . . *Dear Wittgenstein.*

Waterkeeper's Bothy

My deeds are tied up in a family trust
Embracing a salmon river, nightly poached
By sweep-nets, to her ladyship's disgust,
Her private reaches tortuously encroached.

Tucked behind rhododendron palisades
I sheathe you with your mate in a dug-out gloom.
You lumber home at dawn to cast-iron beds,
Trickle of spawn-tanks through a shuttered room.

I'm living in the past, among record fish
She hooked on badger hair, played to her gaff,
Carved for blue-blooded guests on a Ming dish
And immortalized with a game-book epitaph.

While watching, do you poach? With sovereign guile
Beyond reproach, she only skills in style.

Kylemore Castle

Built for a cotton king, who loved the view
Unspoilt by mills, improved by famine's hand
That cleared away people, petrified I grew
Grotesquely rich on mountainous, poor land.

To last for ever, I had to be faced in stone
Dressed by wage-skeletons; a spindly pile
Of storm-grey turrets that defended no one,
And broke my maker, with his fabricated style.

Coming from church to hold her usual place
On Christmas nights, wheeled to the dining-room,
His wife's corpse embalmed in a sealed glass case
Obeyed his command in the brandy-lit gloom.

Now, my linenfold panelled halls retain
In mortmain his dark airs, which nuns maintain.

Tony White's Cottage

Never to be finished was the work he'd planned
When he restored my site, rebuilt the wreck
Of burnt thatch and disbonded walls he'd found
Bleak on a hillock between the ocean and a lake.

A weird huckster had lodged here in the past
Who could cure all diseases; he used to talk
To a dark rock split by lightning; the last
Night he walked out there he never came back.

Always your friend looked forward to being alone
In my raw stone skin, with a wren and a mouse
That crept through random masonry, while a swan
Nested on an island he saw through raindrop glass.

Never to be finished was the life you'd planned
To spend near him. How well he'd understand!

Pier Bar

For donkey's years I've stood in lashing rain
Unbudgingly, casting a fish-hawk eye
On dock-tied hookers. How could we regain
Lost native custom tourist cash would buy?

Snug in my torporific trammelled air
Of a dream village roped to a lifeless quay,
I can help you play with an old craft, but your
Ten-feathered jigs will get fouled up at sea.

What brings you back to me, having said goodbye
To bullhead shillings in my hand-carved till,
Unless to greet, reflected through my dry
Distillery, the dead friend whose glass I fill?

Why drown so carefully with moss-hung chain
On sound moorings? Rig me. I'll entertain.

Miner's Hut

Unused in your desk drawer lies my brass key
To tongue-tied stonework, musky fossil tunes
You've locked away. Come back, not to unmask me
Word for word, but to make me sound in my ruins.

I rose from a desecration of corbelled cells
In holy cashels ringed by the flagellant sea:
Rock taken over by great black-backed gulls
Saluting each other *Sieg Heil,* claiming the sky.

Sink no more mineshafts to bring up fool's gold
With fever. You can't give every spall's lost face
A niche in the anchoretic oratory. Hold
My still-room as a rock pipit's nesting place.

Bring oil to unseize my lock. The lode of ore
To smelt will sound like a fault: wheatear, shearwater.

Hexagon

Three watchful openings of clear plate glass
Give you command of a stormy desolate view
From my hilltop sundial cell as you look across
Dunes, rocks and sea to islands west of Omey.

Six random walls round one all-purpose room
Of calm rupestral concentricity,
With a smell of yeast-bread flowering, enwomb
Your pride in the hermit hut you made of me.

Oak bed, a hundred books, a staunch teak door
And the Twelve Pins of your childhood I include.
No need for you to write. Sun and moon pore
Over curled up flyleaves, brilliantly intrude.

Flood-tide, closing the strand, comes to embrace
Our isolation. Blue arms interlace.

New Forge

From derelict huts of Cleggan rock I grew
To look most natural here, though I began
Strangely: your Breton stone design drawn through
A London architect's Dunfermline plan.

For thirteen years this perfect place to write
Creviced you in my Galway garden bond:
Green Cumbrian slates letting in attic light;
Slieve Donard heather's white cross-border stand.

Why did you sell me? Did you feel trapped here,
Compelled in cold blood to exuviate
My hard pink shell? A Dublin auctioneer
Hammered you free to grow articulate.

Our union was split-level. Now I'm used
To keep old men with infant minds amused.

Cottage for Sale

If you have lost someone you tried to own
Buy me instead. I need to be possessed
For more than seaside weekends: stone by stone
Personified, gaps filled with interest.

Build on my real estate; squander in style
Your passion for belongings; ditch your thought.
Restore old thatch, strip off asbestos tile.
Shape me with love I can't escape, being bought.

Bring children here, and spoil them with my view
Of ocean; burnet roses growing between
Granite outcrops. Let barbed wire renew
Your landbonds. Plant me with a windproof screen.

I'm on the market. Hear my brochure's cry:
Vacant possession, sewn up endlessly.

Horse-Drawn Caravan

My red half-door opens. The mother of nine
Looks at the tip-head where we've stuck, and curses.
'Whenever he took us out of one misfortune
He brought us into another that was worse.'

How many stitches I got, sheltering those two
With their hatchets! They'd slash the skewbald cob
To tread down gaps in hedges we'd go through.
Mostly it was each other's joy they'd rob.

I'd rock like a cradle when they'd start to brawl
Over bottles. Storms did less harm than the pair of them
Spigoting my barrel-top. No luck at all,
No calm until cuckoo slipped into Jerusalem.

If I'm not scrapped sooner, or sold for the price
Of a drink, she'll burn me when the old lad dies.

Old Dispensary

A horse trotting loose, or a cow might stray
By my comatose door. Nobody passed a remark,
All the years I desquamated in decay
Tumorous on the bog-road in the priestly dark.

Now there's a new earth-mover's claw to feed,
The jaws are chewing me over. Neighbours are scared
Because they've heard I'll house a lazy breed
Of verminous, ditch-born tinkers, if repaired.

Let them come, with banners of torn tee-shirts hung
From smashed windows, looks that will turn the milk
Of decent mothers sour. Let my stone sing
With tongues of cant. Let the saintly village sulk.

How can they move me if I keep folk bound
Like spavined jennets padlocked in the pound?

Chalet

No shelter on this site when ocean gales
Assault my cabbage-green school weatherboards:
I stand rebuilt on ground made up of shells,
Dock silt and worms, clay pipes and bog orchids.

Nuns moved me here to install itinerants
With seven children, lost at a district court,
Dumped for their parents' fault in stone-walled convents.
My joinery cramped the family it restored.

Makeshift immobile home, need I be stilted,
Unstable? When my aerial blows down
They kick holes in my roof of mineral felt;
Beg to be changed to a multi-channel town.

Tears, temper, screams, my battered frame endures
By dint of carpentry, no miracle cures.

Prison

Losing your pen in the body-search behind
My dustbin-columned classical façade,
You're led by intercrural routes to find
Your gypsy friend, trussed in my fixed abode.

Before he lost his capricious boyhood, grew
A centaur's beard, hooves, haunches in relief,
Did you cage him with hubristic love? You knew
His touching thievery often gave you life.

Free to face across doubly screened zoo wire,
Stop-watched by warders in a cell, you meet,
Deterred by a faecal smell, beyond desire
Where words fail to regenerate, but cheat.

Poor old people he robbed in bed at night.
What sentence did your teaching help him write?

Wattle Tent

Lobawn, he calls me in shelta, his duck nest
Under a thorn bush on a petering-out lane;
Wattled with hazel cut from the remotest
Copse of a departed ascendancy demesne.

Fourteen lithe rods, carved into wishbones, keep
My head up in the rain. My tarred and buttered
Skin he's smoked and cured. Rats from a trash heap
Steal bits of his begged bread, but he's not bothered.

Thrown back by cheap wine on to his last straw
He finds I can help the pain. His seed has spread
From road to road: boys gathering scrap in new
Pick-ups, girls as young as Juliet wedded.

It dawns on me, when his bantam cock crows,
I'll house him till he dies, wherever he goes.

Newgrange

Brought to a brumal standstill, here I lie
Obliquely floored, mouth curbed by stones that speak
In pick-dressed spirals, egghead sucked bone dry,
Waiting for dawn inside my skull to streak.

Sungod and riverbride died in my bed
To live as bead and elkshorn under earth.
One cairn eye stayed open to feed the dead
A ray of wintry hope, fixed on rebirth.

Up a dark passage, brightening from far back,
A sunbeam seeks my carved leakproof abode.
As pollen dust ignites my pebble stack
The tomb I've made becomes a vivid road.

Once a year it may strike me, a pure gift
Making light work, a mound of greywacke lift.

Friary

Each time you breathe my name – Ross Errilly –
Young leaf-growth rustles in the druid wood,
Felled to convert my land so thoroughly
Stone crosses stand on grass where forest stood.

Here the rain harps on ruins, plucking lost
Tunes from my structure, which the wind pours through
In jackdaw desecration, carping at the dust
And leprous sores my towers like beggars show.

Now my fishponds hold no water. Doors and aisles
Are stacked with donors' tombs, badly invested,
A gift for peeping toms: my lecherous gargoyles
Hacked off by thieves, the bones unresurrected.

Here, too, buried in rhyme, lovers lie dead,
Engraved in words that live each time they're read.

Beehive Cell

There's no comfort inside me, only a small
Hart's-tongue sprouting square, with pyramidal headroom
For one man alone kneeling down: a smell
Of peregrine mutes and eremitical boredom.

Once, in my thirteen hundred years on this barren
Island, have I felt a woman giving birth,
On her own in my spinal cerebellic souterrain,
To a living child, as she knelt on earth.

She crawled under my lintel that purgatorial night
Her menfolk marooned her out of their coracle
To pick dillisk and sloke. What hand brought a light
With angelica root for the pain of her miracle?

Three days she throve in me, suckling the child,
Doing all she had to do, the sea going wild.

Natural Son

Before the spectacled professor snipped
The cord, I heard your birth-cry flood the ward,
And lowered your mother's tortured head, and wept.
The house you'd left would need to be restored.

No worse pain could be borne, to bear the joy
Of seeing you come in a slow dive from the womb,
Pushed from your fluid home, pronounced 'a boy'.
You'll never find so well equipped a room.

No house we build could hope to satisfy
Every small need, now that you've made this move
To share our loneliness, much as we try
Our vocal skill to wall you round with love.

This day you crave so little, we so much
For you to live, who need our merest touch.